Caring For Your Fish

by Mark McPherson

photography by
Marianne Bernstein

Troll Associates

Library of Congress Cataloging in Publication Data

McPherson, Mark (Mark D.)
Caring for your fish.

Includes index.
Summary: Information on how to care for pet fish, from simple goldfish and guppies to more complicated tropical fish.
1. Aquarium fishes—Juvenile literature. 2. Aquariums—Juvenile literature. [1. Aquarium fishes. 2. Aquariums] I. Bernstein, Marianne, ill. II. Title.
SF457.25.M37 1984 639.3'4 84-8563
ISBN 0-8167-0109-1 (lib. bdg.)
ISBN 0-8167-0110-5 (pbk.)

 Printed in the United States of America.
Troll Associates, Mahwah, N.J.

Photo credits: Close-up fish portraits by Aaron Norman. All other photographs by Marianne Bernstein.

The author and publisher wish to thank Crystal Aquariums of New York for their advice and cooperation.

Contents

Goldfish and Guppies 5

Tropical Fish:
Tanks and Equipment 13

Freshwater Tropical Fish 23

Saltwater Tropicals 33

If a Fish Gets Sick 41

Watching Your Fish 45

1

Goldfish and Guppies

The world of fish is large and wonderful. Many different kinds of fish, ranging from tiny guppies to giant bluefish, share the waters of the earth. All breathe by removing oxygen from water with their gills.

Fish kept as pets provide hours of enchantment. They are living creatures so unlike yourself that you can only imagine what their lives are like.

The easiest way to keep fish is to purchase one or two goldfish and a fish bowl. Goldfish are hardy and inexpensive. If you take good care of them, they can live for as long as twenty years.

It's easy to get started. First, purchase a fish bowl, one that has a wide mouth. This allows more contact between the water and the air, which in turn allows more oxygen to dissolve in the water. Like all animals, fish need oxygen to breathe.

Pet stores still sell fish bowls with narrow mouths, so you may have to compare bowls in order to make a good selection.

In addition to a bowl you need a small net to help you remove your fish from the bowl, when necessary. And you will need a siphon hose, a flexible plastic tube. With the hose, you can drain water from the bowl when it needs cleaning.

Feed your goldfish or guppies carefully. Sprinkle only a small amount of food onto the surface of the water.

A goldfish, if you take good care of it, can live ten years or more.

When you have your equipment, you are all ready to select a goldfish. Several varieties of goldfish are available, ranging in price from less than a dollar to several dollars.

Be careful when you buy your goldfish. It is important to get one that is healthy. There are several signs to look for that distinguish a healthy fish from a sick fish.

A healthy fish will be active, and will swim freely and evenly. Its fins will not be damaged. There will be no signs of disease anywhere on its body.

A sick fish may appear sluggish and may stay in one place, at either the top or bottom of the pet-store tank. It may appear to be hiding. A fish that leaves a trail of droppings is sick.

Also, if the pet-store tank contains a number of fish that seem unhealthy, it may be best not to take a fish from that particular tank. The fish in it may all be affected by a disease.

Before you go to buy the goldfish and the fish bowl, carefully rinse out a few plastic jugs (without using soap or detergent). Fill them with tap water. Leave this water out long enough for it to reach room temperature.

Siphon dirty water and debris from your goldfish bowl once a week.

Use this water to fill the fish bowl. Goldfish can handle a wide range of temperatures, but only if the changes are gradual. A sudden change from warm water to cold water may weaken and kill the goldfish.

If you live in an area where chlorine is used to purify drinking water, you should purchase chlorine remover from your pet store. Follow the instructions. Chlorine remover works immediately.

When you buy your goldfish, the salesclerk will put it into a small plastic bag filled with water. Take this plastic bag home right away. It contains only enough oxygen to keep the goldfish alive for a short time.

When you get home, rinse the fish bowl out with water (again, without using soap or detergent). Fill the bowl with water from the plastic jugs that you filled earlier.

When you bring your goldfish home, put it into the fish bowl while it is still inside its water-filled plastic bag.

Place the unopened plastic bag, with your fish inside, into the bowl. Wait a half hour. Waiting allows the water in the bag to gradually reach the same temperature as the water in the bowl. Now you can open the bag and let your fish swim freely in its new home.

Goldfish food consists of bits of dried vegetables. It comes in small boxes and lasts a long time. Once a day, take a tiny bit between your fingers and sprinkle it on the surface of the water. Only if your fish finishes this little bit of food should you sprinkle any more into the bowl.

The reason that you do not give your goldfish a lot of food is simple. Leftover food sinks to the bottom of the bowl and decays. As it decays, it breeds germs that will make your fish sick or cause it to die.

The only other regular responsibility you will have as a goldfish owner is to clean the fish bowl once a week. You need a siphon hose, a bucket, and the plastic jugs you used earlier. Fill the jugs with water the day before you clean the bowl. Place the goldfish bowl on a table. Put one end of the siphon hose in the bowl and the other end of the hose in the bucket, which should be on the floor.

Using the siphon hose like a straw, inhale for just a second on the end of the hose that will go into the bucket. Be careful not to inhale too much, or you will get a mouthful of fish water. Quickly put the end of the hose down into the bucket.

Water will start to flow from the bowl into the bucket. As it does, use the suction of the hose to vacuum dirt from the bottom of the bowl.

Allow the water to continue flowing from the bowl until there is only enough left in the bowl to cover your fish. Then use a damp sponge (*no soap!*) to wipe the inside of the bowl clean. When this is done, refill the bowl with water from the plastic jugs.

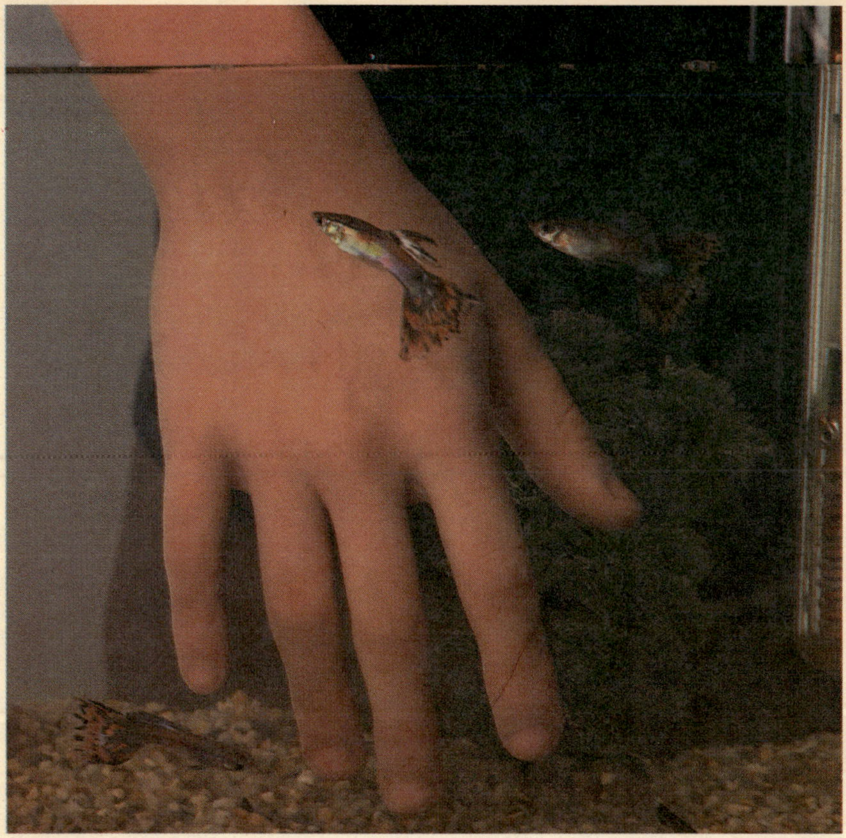

These colorful fancy guppies will produce a large family.

There you have the simplest method of caring for a goldfish. Remember that with proper care goldfish live a long time. If you do a good job, you could have the same fish for ten to twenty years.

After goldfish, the most popular fish kept as pets are guppies. Guppies are small tropical fish that reproduce quickly. Baby guppies are called fry.

The best place to raise guppies is a small fish tank. The tank gives these fish enough room and enough oxygen. Guppy tanks do not necessarily require an electric pump and a filter system (which are discussed in the next chapter).

A pair of guppies, one male and one female, will fill the tank with a dozen or two offspring in a short time. But there is little reason to worry about the guppy population getting out of control. As the tank gets crowded, fewer guppies will be born. And smaller fish will be eaten by larger fish.

Guppies, unlike goldfish, need a constant warm temperature. Their tank should be kept in a place where the temperature will stay above sixty-five degrees at night. During the day, guppies need a temperature between seventy and eighty degrees. If your house gets cold on winter nights, keep a lamp next to the tank or purchase an aquarium heater.

The guppy food sold in pet stores is mostly meat. As with goldfish, sprinkle only a tiny bit on the surface of the water once a day. Wait until this is eaten before sprinkling a little more. Be careful not to overfeed.

Clean the tank once a week with a siphon hose. The inside surface of the glass should be wiped with a damp sponge.

2

Tropical Fish: Tanks and Equipment

If you enjoy goldfish or guppies, then you may want to try caring for tropical fish. Many varieties of tropicals—of many sizes, colors, and temperaments—are available.

All tropical fish, however, fall into one of two categories: those that live in fresh water and those that live in salt water. This chapter covers most of the basic elements of keeping all tropicals, but focuses on freshwater fish. The next chapter discusses saltwater fish.

The first step toward owning tropical fish is the purchase of a fish tank. A ten-gallon tank is the smallest size you should consider. No tank will appear as large as it did when empty, once you have added the equipment, plants, gravel, and decorations. Tanks larger than ten gallons are even better. But, of course, as size increases, so does price.

When you purchase the tank, you should also purchase other necessary equipment. You will need all or most of the following:

- hood and light unit

- filter and pump

Swordtails are always sold as a male and female pair.

To set up your tank, arrange gravel on an incline.

Next, cover the gravel with a few sheets of newspaper.

Fill the tank by pouring water onto the newspaper, which will rise with the water level. The carefully arranged gravel will remain in place.

When the tank is more than half full, add plants and rocks.

- air stone, air pump, plastic tubing, and three-way valve
- heater and thermostat
- thermometer
- scraper
- pH test and balance kit

This is a long list, but each item on it is important to an aquarium set-up. Let's look closely at the role each plays.

Hood and light unit. The hood contains the fluorescent light, and the light makes the aquarium plants grow and prosper. The hood itself serves two other purposes. It prevents water from evaporating from the tank, and it prevents lively fish from jumping out of the tank.

Filter and pump. The filter cleans and freshens the water in the tank. You put activated charcoal and dacron fluff inside the filter to help accomplish this. The pump, which often comes as part of the filter unit, runs the filter. It is plugged into an electrical outlet, but uses very little electricity.

Air stone and air pump. The air stone releases air bubbles into the aquarium. Bubbles help remove carbon dioxide from the water, and are also nice to look at. The air pump sends air to the air stone.

Plastic tubing and three-way valve. These connect the air pump with the air stone.

Heater. The heater works best if it has an automatic thermostat. The thermostat keeps the water at the proper temperature (seventy to eighty degrees).

Important aquarium equipment includes: (top) filter and pump unit; (center, left to right) heater, thermometer, air pump; (bottom) air stone with plastic hose.

Thermometer. The thermometer keeps track of the temperature. If the temperature gets too high or too low, you must adjust the thermostat accordingly.

Scraper. You use the scraper to remove algae from

the inside surface of the tank.

pH test and balance kit. You use this kit to test the water for pH, which is a measurement of the balance of acidity and alkalinity. The kit contains chemicals that you can add to the tank to correct this balance, if necessary. Most of the pH kits available work by adding a chemical to a small test tube containing water from the tank. The chemical causes the water to change color. This color is then compared to colors on a chart that comes with the kit.

Once your tank and equipment are in order, you can begin decorating the tank. The three things that most people use to create the underwater world of the aquarium are gravel, rocks, and plants.

Gravel. Gravel comes in many colors. It should cover the bottom of the aquarium, so the roots of your underwater plants can be secure and supported. Then the plants will stay upright and where you place them. Buy gravel from the pet store. Rinse it thoroughly. With your parents' help, boil the gravel in a large pot of water to kill bacteria and microorganisms. Then drain and dry the gravel before you place it on the bottom of the tank.

Rocks. Attractive rocks add to the beauty of an aquarium. Rocks also provide hiding and breeding places for fish. Generally, it is best to buy rocks from the pet store, and only rocks intended for aquarium use. These will not affect the chemical balance of the water. Just as with gravel, boil the rocks in a pot before placing them in the tank.

Plants. Next to the fish themselves, plants do the most to turn your aquarium into a real and beautiful underwater world. The fish occasionally nibble on them for food. Plants also release oxygen into the water and, like rocks, serve as hiding and breeding places for the fish.

Now that you know about all the things needed for your aquarium, you are ready to begin setting it up.

Install the aquarium equipment before filling the tank completely.

Setting Up

Before you set up your new fish tank, make sure that you have a sturdy table or stand on which to place it. Water is quite heavy. It weighs over eight pounds per gallon, so a ten-gallon tank will weigh more than eighty pounds when full. A twenty-gallon tank will weigh more than one hundred and sixty pounds.

Once the aquarium tank is settled on a steady surface, you can begin adding the equipment and decorations. If you've chosen the kind of filter that goes under the gravel, put this down first. If not, begin by pouring the sand or gravel into the bottom of the tank. Arrange the gravel so that it slopes down a few inches from the back to the front of the tank. This encourages dirt to settle in the front area, making it easier to get at when you clean the tank.

Now you can fill the tank with water, about four-fifths of the way to the top. Do not pour the water directly onto the gravel that you have so carefully arranged. Cover it with newspapers and then pour the water on top of these. This prevents the gravel from washing out of position. As you fill the tank, the newspapers will rise to the surface. When the tank is half full, remove the newspapers and discard them.

With the tank filled halfway, add the plants and rocks. Push the roots of each plant down into the gravel a few inches from where you want the plant to be. Then move the plant through the gravel to its position. This helps to insure that the roots will be anchored firmly below the surface of the gravel. Arrange the rocks so that they look nice with the plants.

After you have placed the plants and rocks, install your filter, heater, and air stone. Try to conceal each of these behind plants or rocks.

Now fill the tank to about an inch below the top and wait at least a day before you introduce fish into the aquarium. A day's wait gives the water a chance to reach room temperature and allows dissolved chlorine to escape. Some aquarium keepers recommend waiting a whole week before putting in the fish. This allows the plants to take root without being disturbed by the fish. Also, test the

Test the pH (acid-alkali balance) of the aquarium water once or twice a week. If the balance is off, add chemicals to correct it.

pH after the first day, and adjust it so that it is close to the pH of the tanks in the pet store where you get your fish. (Ask the pet-store manager at what pH level they keep their tanks.)

The aquarium is now ready. The fish can be purchased from the pet store and brought home. They will be in small plastic bags. Remember, do not open the bags and dump the fish into the tank right away. A rapid temperature change usually kills tropical fish.

Put the bags in the tank unopened. It should take a half-hour or an hour for the water inside the bags to reach the same temperature as that of the water in the tank. When the temperatures are the same, open the bags and let the fish swim out into their new home.

3

Freshwater Tropical Fish

Any large pet- or aquarium-supply center offers a wide variety of tropical fish. The fish are available at prices ranging from less than a dollar to several dollars. When you go to the store, be sure to know how much you can spend so that you can select fish that will fit into your budget.

Write down a list of the fish you want and show the list to a salesperson. Ask the salesperson to go over your selections. He or she can tell you if you have picked two or more types of fish that do not get along well together in the same tank. Some fish are aggressive—they may attack and eat other fish.

When you select fish, take your time and study the different fish in each tank. Some will be slow, steady swimmers. Some will be fast, darting swimmers. Some like to hide near rocks. Some will hover near the bottom of the tank. Others will glide along the surface of the water. Still others will join together in groups, called schools, made up of one type of fish.

Pick the fish you can afford that most appeal to you. But also consider useful fish—like the many varieties of catfish—that will help keep your tank clean by eating waste from the bottom.

If you want to avoid fish that become sick easily,

When you bring home your tropical fish, introduce them to the aquarium while they are still inside plastic bags from the pet store.

After all the hard work of setting up your aquarium, you can now look forward to many hours of wonderful fish-gazing.

ask the salesclerk to recommend those that are known to be hardy. And always check to make sure that the fish you buy appear healthy.

A healthy fish swims freely and evenly, and does not look sluggish. Make sure there are no signs of disease on the fish. A common sign is white spots. Another sign is a trail of droppings at the fish's tail. Just as with goldfish and guppies, avoid buying a fish from a tank in which you see any fish that appear to be sick. You may take home what seems to be a healthy fish and wind up exposing the entire population of your aquarium to sickness. A well-run aquarium-supply store will not allow sick fish to remain in a tank with other fish.

Finally, point out to the salesclerk the specific fish you want, and make sure that those are the fish you get.

Feeding

The most important part of caring for tropical fish is feeding them. Do this every day and do it carefully. First-time fish owners often think that fish need a lot of food. They don't. Most tropical fish will eat their fill on the small amount of food that you give them. Other fish, particularly catfish, will eat mostly the food available to them on the bottom and sides of the tank—algae, waste, and leftovers.

There are two ways to handle daily feedings. One method calls for a single meal each day. The other way calls for two or three lighter meals in a day. The concern is not that fish will eat too much, but that they will not finish the food they are given. Leftover food decays, settles in the

The Ramirez' Dwarf Cichlid, or "Ram."

This catfish is a scavenger. It helps keep an aquarium clean.

Neon Tetras are "schooling" fish—they swim together in groups.

tank, and breeds bacteria that are dangerous to the fish. So give the fish only as much as they are able to eat completely in a few minutes.

For tropical fish, use both dried and live food. Many brands of boxed, dried food are available, each containing slightly different mixtures and ingredients. Pick up three or four brands and use a different one each day. This helps to provide your fish with a varied and balanced diet.

The Siamese Fighting Fish, or "Betta," may be the most colorful freshwater tropical fish.

The Clown Loach is a large, playful fish that is happiest when it has a companion of its own kind.

Live food is not much harder to use than dried food, and it is especially good for tropical fish. The two most popular types of live food are brine shrimp and tubifex worms. Aquarium-supply stores usually sell both of these. The salesclerk can explain to you how to feed them to your fish.

A good variety of different brands of dried food, and the inclusion of live food, will provide your fish with an excellent diet.

Cleaning the Aquarium

It is important to clean your aquarium thoroughly every ten days to two weeks. You might, for instance,

A Bleeding-Heart Tetra.

A Dwarf Gourami.

want to reserve every other Saturday morning or afternoon for this task.

Start out by filling several plastic gallon jugs with fresh water. It is best to do this the day or night before so that the water reaches room temperature. This also allows any chlorine dissolved in the water to escape. If you do not leave the water out overnight, add a few drops of chlorine remover before pouring the water into the tank.

Clean the tank by using a siphon hose. Remove about a third of the water in the aquarium. At the same time, "vacuum" dirt from the bottom of the tank. Push the end of the siphon hose below the surface of the gravel, and move the hose around the whole area of the bottom of the tank. Some gravel will be taken away as well, but this can be washed and returned to the tank.

Clean your aquarium with a siphon hose every two weeks.

Make sure that you use a scraper to remove algae that can grow on the inside glass.

If there are large rocks in your aquarium, move these by hand and vacuum the area beneath them. If plants are uprooted, don't be too concerned. You can replant them. A clean tank is more important than the plants. And try to keep the siphon away from the fish, or they will get a ride through the hose.

While the water level is low, use a damp, clean, soapless sponge to wipe the exposed glass inside the tank. Then refill the tank with water from the plastic jugs that you filled in advance.

The combination of replacing a third of the water and cleaning the tank thoroughly will keep the aquarium environment fresh and healthy.

4

Saltwater Tropicals

Caring for tropical fish that live in salt water is more difficult than keeping freshwater fish. The risk of pollution and disease is greater. And maintaining the chemical balance of the aquarium can be complicated.

A fish tank that is set up for saltwater fish is called a marine aquarium. Some hobbyists prefer marine aquariums, because saltwater fish species are more colorful than freshwater species.

One of the first things to consider is the size of the tank. Small tanks are easily polluted when used as marine aquariums. You should, therefore, start out with a twenty- or twenty-five-gallon tank.

To fight pollution in a marine aquarium, two filters are recommended. Use both a sub-sand filter and an out-of-tank filter. Both are standard equipment, sold at aquarium-supply stores.

Next, you must make salt water. Do this by adding packaged salt mixtures sold in pet stores to the ordinary tap water with which you have filled your tank. It is possible to use salt water directly from the ocean, but you will probably not have this option unless you live near the beach.

When adding salt mixtures to an aquarium, you will need a hydrometer. A hydrometer measures a property of water known as *specific gravity*. It is not important to understand this property. All you have to know is that

The Orange-Lined Triggerfish (top), and the Powder-Blue Tang (bottom), are two beautiful saltwater tropicals.

The Filament Butterflyfish.

enough salt must be added to make the hydrometer read 1.025.

Once this reading is achieved, do not add more salt when the water level in the tank drops because of evaporation. It is only the water that evaporates, not the salt.

Marine aquariums require several chemical tests, in addition to the pH tests that are done in freshwater aquariums. The salesclerk at your aquarium-supply center can tell you the tests that you need to purchase, and how and when they should be used.

A Long-Nose Hawkfish.

An Anemonefish.

The feeding of saltwater tropical fish is similar to the feeding of freshwater fish. Select a few different brands of dried food, and switch from one to another on different days. Supplement these with "live" foods, such as brine shrimp. Let your pet-store clerk suggest other live foods for saltwater fish. A varied diet is the healthiest.

 A Catalina Goby.

A Sweet Lips.

Overfeeding is even more dangerous in a marine aquarium than in a freshwater tank. This is because of the stronger tendency for disease and pollution to occur in the marine aquarium.

Marine aquariums are decorated differently than freshwater aquariums. Live plants, for instance, should not be used in your first attempt to set up and keep a marine aquarium. It will be difficult to keep them alive. Instead, corals make beautiful decorations.

Corals suitable for marine aquariums can be purchased from pet stores or aquarium-supply stores. If coral is taken from the sea, it must be soaked in bleach first, then soaked in water to rinse off the bleach. The same applies to coral purchased in gift shops. However, if the gift-shop coral has been colored with a dye, it should not be used at all.

An Anemonefish swims through a Sea Anemone.

A starfish makes an attractive addition to any marine aquarium.

Whole seashells should not be used for decorating marine aquariums. Sometimes these shells contain bits of the animals that once lived in them, and as a result they become places where disease can grow. Pieces of *broken* sea shells are far safer, but even these must be boiled before they are put into an aquarium.

Fish are not the only creatures that can live in marine aquariums. Starfish and sea urchins make attractive guests. Both are easy to care for, and they are not often victims of disease or parasites. Starfish have the amazing capability to regrow a "limb," should one be cut off or eaten.

5

If a Fish Gets Sick

If you have done everything possible to keep your tank healthy, your fish should not be troubled too often by disease. But occasionally you will be confronted with a sick fish.

The most important thing to do when you spot a sick fish is to remove it from the aquarium and put it into a separate, smaller tank. Separation helps keep the illness from spreading to other fish. And if the fish should die, it will not pollute the main tank if it decays before you've had a chance to remove it.

Also, once you have placed the sick fish in a separate tank, you will be able to treat it more effectively with medicine.

A common disease that attacks tropical fish is "Ick." Ick is a parasite that appears on the fish as tiny white spots. If left untreated, these spots become the breeding ground for other diseases, most commonly a white, cottony fungus. Aquarium-supply stores sell cures for both of these diseases as well as for others.

Another problem for tropical fish is fin rot, which is often caused if a fin has been bitten and damaged in a fight with another fish. Fin rot is remedied by applying a thin coat of Mercurichrome, available at drug stores, to the damaged fin.

Remember that you should never touch a fish when your hands are dry. Wet them first. This will prevent

The most frequent disease that strikes tropical fish is called "Ick," for short. It can lead to a fungus infection that shows up as a cottony white patch on the fish.

Check hiding places in the tank for fish that might be sick.

a disturbance of the protective, slimy coating that covers the fish's body. Should this slimy coating be disturbed, disease and death can result.

If you are a careful observer of your aquarium, you will notice sick fish before it is too late to treat them. Once you get them into your "hospital" tank, you can treat them with medicine. Always remember to follow these rules:

1) Make sure that your hospital tank is the same temperature as the main aquarium. If treatment of the disease requires raising the temperature, do this gradually.
2) When using medicine, follow the directions on the package exactly.

3) Make sure that the fish is completely well before returning it to the main tank. This may require that you gradually lower the temperature of the hospital tank, if you had to raise it to treat the disease.
4) Avoid ever touching a fish, but if you must, make sure that your hands are wet.

Being a good fish doctor is part of owning a tropical-fish aquarium. It will make the difference that results in a healthy, flourishing underwater world.

6
Watching Your Fish

With your aquarium in full operation, you can expect to have many fascinating hours of fish watching. You will discover many things as you sit in front of the tank.

Each type of fish will behave differently—in the way it swims, how it relates to other fish, and where it most likes to be in the aquarium environment.

One of the first things you can learn is which fish are the leaders in the tank. This will be most obvious at feeding time. The dominant fish will control the area where you place the food, and they will tend to chase other, less powerful fish away.

At first your fish might become nervous when you are watching them, but gradually they will get used to you. You should avoid tapping on the glass, especially at first. But as your fish instinctively begin to be aware that you are not a threat to them, many of them may react positively to a very light tapping on the glass and the upper edge of the tank.

You will notice that smaller fish, particularly those that swim in schools, like to hide among the plants and near rocks. They feel safer in these places.

If you put the tip of your finger in the water, you will notice that some fish stay away. Some, however, try to bite at your finger as though it were food, and others swim around it in a friendly manner.

At feeding time, you will also notice unusual differences. Some fish will eat right at the water's surface.

The Algae-Eater is forever at work, helping to keep glass and gravel algae-free.

Others will wait for the food to fall to the mid-tank area. And some fish will raid the feeding area in an almost hostile manner, grabbing food and quickly swimming away with it.

Still other fish pay no attention to the food at all. Some of these fish eat only the leftovers that have already fallen to the bottom of the tank. Others eat only the algae that grows on the rocks and on the inside surface of the tank.

You will find the experience of watching your fish fun and educational. The work that you must put into an aquarium will be rewarded by your pride in creating and maintaining a beautiful underwater world.

INDEX

Behavior of fish, observing 45–47
  feeding behavior, 45–46

Disease, 41–43
  fin rot, 41
  how to treat, 41–43
    rules for treatment, 42–43
  "Ick," 41

"Fish watching," 45–47
freshwater aquarium
  cleaning, 28–31
  equipment for, 13–17
  setting up, 18–21
freshwater tropical fish, 23–31
  feeding, 25–28
  selecting, 23–24

Goldfish, 5–10
  bowl
    cleaning, 9
    selecting, 5
    setting up, 7–9
  feeding, 9
  food, 9
  selecting, 6–7
guppies, 5, 10–11
  breeding, 11
  feeding, 11
  tank for, 10
    cleaning, 11
  water temperature for, 11

"Hospital" tank, 42

Marine aquarium (for saltwater tropical fish), 33–39
  chemical tests of, 34
  decorating, 37–39
  filters for, 33
  salt water for, 33–34
  size, 33

Saltwater tropical fish, 33–39
  feeding, 36–37
sea urchins, 39
siphon (hose), 5
  cleaning goldfish bowl with, 9
  how to use, 9
starfish, 39

Tropical fish, 13–39
  tank for, 13
    equipment, 13–17
    setting up, 18–21